BLUE JUNE

JOHN DOMINIC NAZARETH

INDIA • SINGAPORE • MALAYSIA

realized that he might prefer verbal over written communication. He enjoyed talking in allegories.-

His primary school teachers and my grandparents were the first to identify a difference in the way he wrote and drew. The geometry class was a nightmare in middle school, and we noticed that he always had an atypical strained grip on his drawing pencils. He developed an illegible writing which could not be improved. This was not clear early on, as he had no difficulty playing badminton, cricket or swimming. Though he was recognized as a poet in school, his bad handwriting was always highlighted at every parent teacher meeting.

When we attended school, there was no concept of a special educator then or a pathway to assess and support children with special needs. Although he possessed a high IQ, excelling particularly in language and the humanities, his writing greatly deterred his scores. He was denied a scribe in the examinations then. He lost a possible career in Social sciences, Literature and Journalism.

His long battle with mood swings began at this time, which further hampered his education in Degree College. Despite his troubles, he took solace in music, games and books like The Holy Bible, current affairs, sports journals and Philosophy. He was cheerful and never lost his faith in God. He continued to write both poetry and prose, but he could not handle a typewriter or computer as his fingers were always slow and coordination of finger movements was a challenge. At that time, we were not able to arrive at what caused the stiffness, being diagnosed as a fine motor disability many years later. I do remember my mother trying various other activities to count as rehabilitation, but it was not effective. With her encouragement, he volunteered at the local Seminary, which was close to our house to correct English papers. He also taught informal spoken English to primary school children in the vicinity and volunteered at the India Every Home Crusade as a translator. Inspired by a friend, he developed a new interest in ethnology, while attending the Anglo-Indian Association meetings and continued to do his research on the Anglo Indian community. John always assisted my mother with daily shopping and volunteered to distribute bread to the poor.

My mother's death hit John very hard. On the advice of his doctor, he attended seventeen months of rehabilitation at the Medico Pastoral Association, Bangalore and learnt the program which has done wonders for thousands. Here he learnt to overcome his challenges, accept his disability as a stepping stone to success and embark on his journey of hope. He progressed in his daily living activities, as he realized that he was blessed with other talents like poetry and music which he could harness. It was then he decided to write a few lines daily and his poems took shape in the form of this book. Cheering the elderly and always showing kindness to the poor and marginalized were his innermost talents and gifts that he shares as a noble giver.

John is an inspiration for all of us at home, as he has been a loving sibling, spreading joy to the family and the elderly. His strength comes from great faith in God and a belief in the divine plan for each one. He is an inspiration for all who have suffered from similar challenges.

GITHA REBELLO,

Third sister

FOREWORD

I am delighted to recommend BLUE JUNE, a collection of beautiful poems by John Nazareth. I have known John as well as his family for a long time. John being the last-born son after four daughters, a very privileged position in any Indian family, is a multi-talented person. He has been able to overcome his disabilities by his creativity and has found meaning and purpose in life by his poetry. The poems highlight his life's experiences and are grouped based on their content into faith, nature, reflections, relationship and more. I am sure that John's poetry will be soothing and therapeutic to a lot of people.

Being a mental health professional myself and having spent a whole lifetime career in this line, in my opinion I believe that the intricate relationship between creativity, poetry, music, and mental health are closely linked. Numerous studies have highlighted the prevalence of mental ill health among artists, writers, musicians, and other creative persons. Stories related to the struggles of the great German composer Beethoven, the Dutch painter Vincent Van Gogh, American poet and novelist Sylvia Plath and many other creative geniuses are well known. There is growing evidence that art, music, and poetry can also be very therapeutic for various kinds of illnesses.

I wish all the readers an enjoyable experience with this creative anthology of poems by John Nazareth.

Dr. Mohan K Isaac

Clinical Professor of Psychiatry,

The University of Western Australia &

Former Head, Department of Psychiatry, National Institute of Mental Health and Neurosciences

Bangalore, India

INTRODUCTION

Poetry can heal our life's wounds. It is a double edge sword. Poetry involves solemn music and gushing humor. My poems speak of my life, my thoughts and my journey through lyrical growth, social (prose) rhythm and biblical Influence I had written poems in my teens which have been sadly lost; however, the poems I wrote after 2003, were collated into this booklet and thus these are my latter reflections

ACKNOWLEDGEMENTS

Mum and Dad

My Deepest gratitude to my father Wilfred Nazareth who taught me the basics of English poetry and to my late mother Rita Nazareth who inspired in me love for poetry. My sisters, uncles, aunts and cousins who drew in me and filled me with poetry. My school teachers and college Lecturers and friends who encouraged me. The many medical doctors and counselors who carefully listened to and built in me cogent insights. Finally I want to thank all those who volunteered to type for me as I could never use a keyboard due to my slow fingers.

Grandparents

PERSPECTIVES

My change from sinner to Saint through the gift of faith is expressed in these perspectives. Many are the cause for my inspiration. Jesus Christ and the English legends John Keats, John Milton, Henry Derozio and Thomas Gray to name a few. I am also fond of Sarojini Naidu, Toru Dutt, Alfred Tennyson and William Wordsworth.

Jesus quickly builds the body of Christ among his people by the finished work on the cross. Nee-Toh-Sheng wrote Chinese Poetry in English .His Motto was Love and Laugh. Alfred Kroeber wrote Poems on Creative Minorities. King David in the Old Testament wrote Psalms. So I also made my pen mightier than the sword. Poetry can be either rough or sublime. It brings about social freedom. Robert Southey's " The Battle of Blenheim " in which Jesus Christ is Divine Being (God) and Social Being (Man) are genres which inspire me.

I was heart-broken having lost my dear mother in 2003. Another tragic event that saddened me was the hundred feet Tsunami in the year 2004 that took many lives and caused damage to land and property around the Indian sub-continent. This calamity shook me and I had a very close experience of

God –Jesus Christ. His greatness and power made me realize, "What is man before God?" "We are nothing".

A new spirit of humility arose within me. I began to contemplate more about who I really am and my purpose in this planet. My mother's strong faith and upbringing revived my spirit towards God the giver of Life. I spent a brief span of seventeen months at Medico Pastoral Association to recover and gain life skills and social skills and become an overcomer. It was here that I understood myself better and accepted my disability of slow fingers and other short comings. I decided to Praise God through singing and praying daily and began wielding my pen to write poetry.

FAITH POEMS

1. SERVICE

Service brings to life true love
It flows with inner joy above

Service has many great shades
From sin it never ever fades

Service brings to fellow men
Echoes of hues now and then

Heaven's beacon light shines bright when
We draw nigh to our fellow men

And shines most radiant still
When to none do we bear ill

For in communing to our kin
We move away from the lure of sin

And rising profound from it
Bear loving grace within

2. JESUS DIVINE

Jesus is our sacred design
Jesus is our flame divine

Jesus is divinely found
Jesus is great and profound

Jesus is absolute solitude
Jesus is generous to the multitude

Life is being noble and wise
Blest in joyful belief to arise

Life is full of noble design
Finding one's calling divine

Noble design is joyful flock
Jesus is our eternal Rock

3. FLAME

With fervor does my soul burn
And for Jesus alone crave
With passion does my spirit yearn
The peace of Jesus to save
In me stirs a flame divine
A flame shared and yet mine

At Mysore as a toddler and Chitra celebrating her
5th birthday

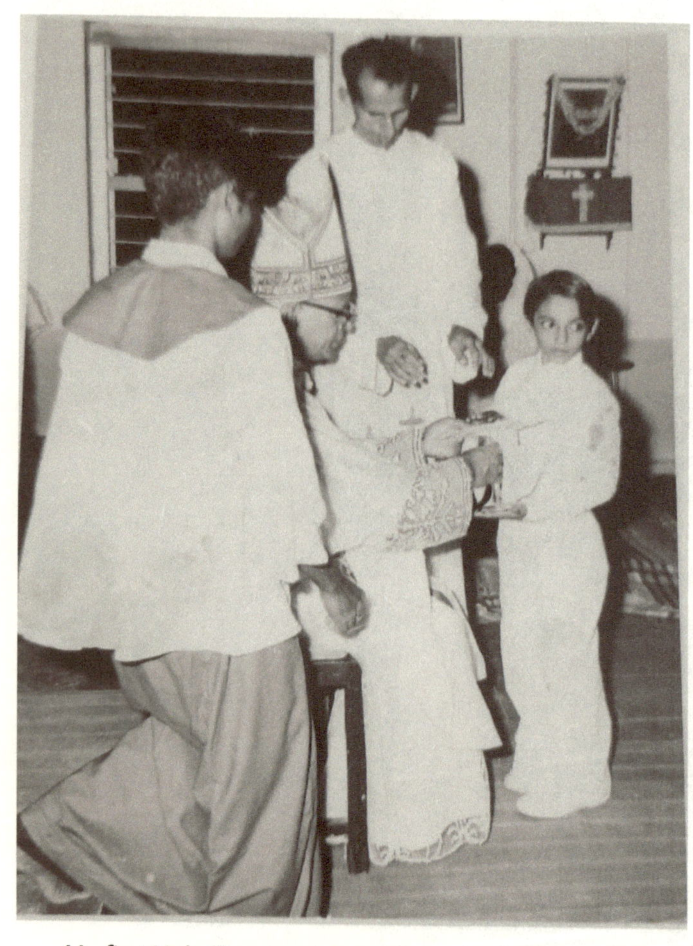

My first Holy Communion at Munirabad July 7, 1977

4. INNERSELF

My inner life is spent with care,
And there blows a little listless air

Around me; but yet I fully place
My boundless faith in divine grace

And there initiates deep within
The blissful union of Yang and Yin

And my spirit calls ever anew
To the Spirit yonder so true.

5. JOURNEY

We have journeyed with the great;
Miles have we onward trod!
Beholding the design of fate;
Witnessing the hand of God
And the great have led us far-
And there shone for us the star,
That once shone over Bethlehem:
Now we must journey far within,
And discover bereft of our sin-
In each one a truly radiant gem.

6. THE INNER CALL

The cleansing inner call does spring
From the most interior source
The self in query does do ring
As it runs its full course

And the bliss which strikes our eyes
From our fall we jubilantly rise
Makes us with the spirit commune
And with nature gaily attune

7. PLEASURE AND PAIN

Between pleasure and pain
Lies unexplored terrain
Which might in words flout
But in life shall be about
Which ancient Indian sages
Have shared Freudian images.

Between pleasure and pain
Lies grim reality strain
Which straddles worlds two
And lies open to a few.
A silken bliss of solitude
Where truth is best viewed.

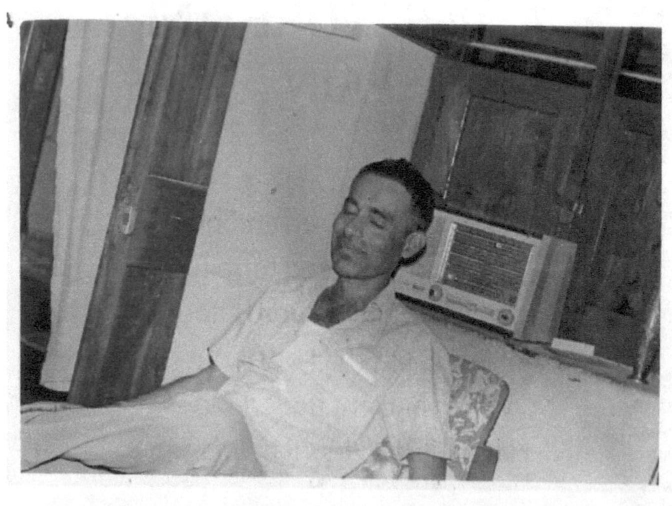

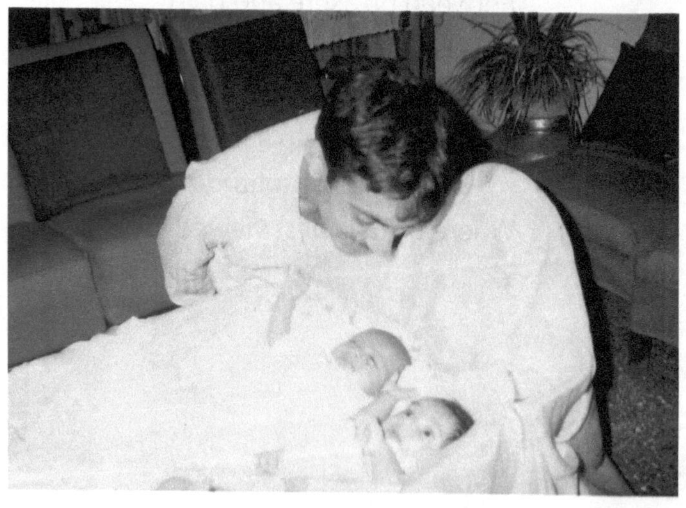

8. BLISS

Bliss is but that inwardness
That leads from joy to joy in vain
The soul must in time regress
To immerse itself in deeper pain

Bliss is but that inwardness
That refuses in fully glorious style
The lure of sin in socialness
And holds sway like a splendid isle!

9. THE INNER VOICE

Silence in space flows
Love with time grows

Innocence builds the voice
For the child to rejoice

When he steps into life's void
And knows which task to avoid.

10. CHRISTMAS

Jesus Christ at Christmas dawn
In humble manger of Virgin born

First Light gleamed as Love glows
Word of God as divine child arose

The birth of our savior and life
Christmas heals our daily strife.

11. SEASON OF LENT

This lovely life so lovely spent
Is forever meaningful in Lent

The Holy Bible divinely felt
Our perpetual sins shall melt

This passion of Christ felt
Truth and Grace well spelt

12. JOYFUL DREAM

Joyful Virgin, Virgin divine
Joyful Mary, Virgin mine

Joyful Virgin, Virgin flight
Joyful Mary, Virgin delight

Joyful Virgin, Virgin been
Joyful Mary, Virgin queen

Raichur 1975

13. SETTLED

We are a settled flock
And most settled belong
This is the story fully strong
Jesus Christ is our rock
This is indeed our life's tale
Shall we begin so to fail?

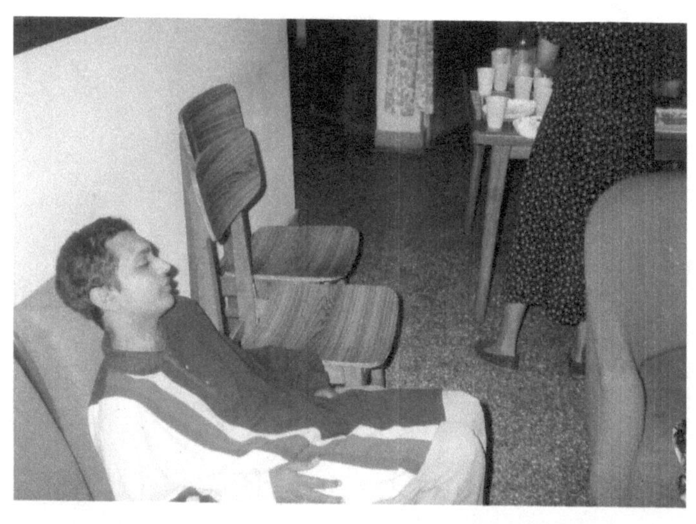

14. SUBTLE

Our Dreams rose and fell
Our Dreams began to swell

Life defers but is subtle
Honest methods will settle

Life builds hues stable
Joyful Virgin grows fable

Life is its most placid
But basic gist of twist

Builds away the rancid
Basic life in Christ

We battle with flames
And the gift and claims

Our exquisite fashion
Full of hurt passion

15. QUICK FIELD

Great life is Quick Field
Jesus Christ is our Rock

Delicate enough to wield
Us from both grief and shock

Quick field is just well slick
Truth shall finally click

16. JOY IS LIFE

Joy is life, Joy is glow and Joy makes us grow
Oh! That your presence fills us with Joy
You Lord are our dwelling place to rejoice

17. NOTICE AND LOVE

Just notice joy and grief
Just notice life that is brief

Life is great, Life is gold
Life is both hot and cold

Just notice Jesus Christ
Just notice the Holy Spirit

Jesus Christ is just love
Life builds us from above

Jesus Christ is Risen Glory
Bliss builds song and story

Just Love is full of blends
Passion for foes and friends

Just notice sacred design
Just notice flame divine

18. FALSE BLAME

When just laid with false blame
Gentle and quick do we abide
Shall make Jesus Christ reside
In His time He will acclaim
Jesus Christ our Light Divine
Rushed of full belief mine

19. LIFE BUILDS

Rosy Blue is life beside
That in full glory glide

Clear joys of the Risen King
Shock and grief bring

Life is purple gate
Soft and rough fate

Life builds love Claims
Life guilds love flames

Jesus Christ grows life
Jesus Christ Flows Life

Choice in being is clear
Choice in being is dear

20. LIFE'S CALL

Jesus build's my life's call
Fill's me with rich love for all

His Full gentle mercy Flows
And shared wealth grows

To heal and to forgive
That all might strongly live

21. EASTER

57

Joyful Flock at Easter Glory
Joyful Flock of Easter Gifts
Jesus Christ of Passion Story
Jesus Christ on Calvary Lifts

Joyful Flock at Jaffa built
Joyful Flock heals False Guilt
Joyful being has its grief
Joyful being is most brief

Joyful being is Jaffa built
Joyful being is without guilt
Joyful being at Calvary
Joyful being is Liberty

22. ABOUT BLISS

Bliss fills! Bliss grows
The ethnic clock flows

Jesus Christ is Lord
Bliss fills The Word

This will fulfill change
Life is clear and strange

Grief is no more grief
Joy tale is seldom brief

Joy grows magic blend
Life is our lovely Friend

23. CHANGE

Old Habits just die hard
Most people cease to explore
New habits is the social card
Fabian rights to Fabian score

Old Habits most often die slow
New Habits just gleam and grow
Fulfill Change Fulfill flow
Jesus Christ built his glow

Life at best is fulfill change
Life is subtle, Life is strange
Choice indeed is full Stream
Chance and Change is dream

24. JOYFUL BELLS

Joyful Bells ring loud and clear
Joyful Bells from far and near

Jesus Christ shed blood to save
And we his Joyful flock are brave

Life is daily clock to flow
Rich roles and role rush glow

At Aunty Rose's wedding Mangalore 1973

25. LIFE FLOCK

63

Jesus Life Jesus Flock
Full of great Love Flock

Jesus Exist Jesus Flock
Life abundant is Christ Flock

Jesus life Jesus Flock
Love abounds in Christ Flock

26. JOYFUL
ECHOES

Life is love at refuse
When wild with global values

Holy chimes do qualify
Jaffa at climax to sigh

Bible filled Jesus Christ
Sprang to quench all thirst.

Live soft with love in refuse
The global passion of soft abuse

The refusing that gleams wild
That seldom burns in a fond child

Jesus Christ sketches the refuse
With Joyful echoes that bring us blues.

27. PRECIOUS BLOOD

Precious Blood of Jesus is Holy Stock
Precious Blood of Jesus is Joyful Flock

Precious Blood of Jesus is living Stream
Precious Blood of Jesus is Divine Dream

Precious Blood of Jesus is Miracle Grasp
Precious Blood of Jesus is Favoured Class

28. RICH ROLE

Role Lock is just doing work
Fluid and Swift just doing
Bible-Built Jesus full shock
Life is gold hush just being
Role Lock is sinuous gleam
Golden chance to its dream

Role Jell builds fresh role gifts
Swift and fluid dream that lifts
Builds slight blue rain blend
Global planet that frail flows
Special flames of Great friend
Roll Jell of Jesus that Grows

Role Rush is Role Rush
Jesus Christ is of Blush
Rich Role is joyful glow
Jesus Christ bled to flow
Bold and Strong Jubilee
Bread and Wine at Galilee.

Rich Roles juggle glow
Jesus Christ bled flow
He is the perpetual gate
Silken king of full fate
Rich Roles like a stream
In its great bright gleam

Risen Glory of Globe
Jesus Christ in Robe
Life –hued on Cross
Church Clock on Cross

29. MARY

Mary who justly loves
Meek and mild she moves

Mary-source of full light
To radiate enough delight

With full glory she glows
Mary often gently echoes

NATURE POEMS

My early childhood years were spent in a camp on the banks of the river Tungabhadra. The river, rocks and hills and canals with gardens are my inspiration. Different shades of nature have inspired my poems. I attempted to write poetry in class-6. This was on a rock behind the Bethany Sisters Convent on the way to School.

My friend Khader Ali Khan used to write Urdu poetry and I would write in English along with a classmate and close friend Althea Mitchell Garman. The rock at Benson Town was the fun place where we would unload our school bags and attempt poetry under the trees. Later in high school I was recognized for this talent.

1. MOTHER PLANET

Great studies on planet Earth
Great symbols of such bliss and mirth

Social gleams of nature's bounty
Glorious gift of mother plenty

The clock of belief and blame
Mother planet is a flame

2. PEBBLES

72

The blue stream is bright in glow
Soft shade and clear in its flow

It strikes in its most vivid gleam
Like bright pebbles in the stream

Blue streams that flow out of blue nails
The best shade of Red Hot Trails

3. HILLS

Life has its Rosy billows
The black face of grassy willows

Gleams of golden hills and vales
Streams that strike its silken tales

Claims of great and grand hues
Foils of lovely lilting fuse

4. RIVER

Like the rushing river
In its sinuous gleam
Holds the twisted shiver
Of its brightest dream
By the river Tunga I felt
Golden dreams to melt

RELATIONSHIP POEMS

Relationship poems were the most challenging for want of words. The poem on my mother is a Eulogy I wrote on her death. To write about the beauty in my near and dear family who have loved me was a beautiful experience, because I owe my existence to my dearest family.

Mum and my four sisters

1. MOTHER
(RITA NAZARETH)

Great Sister dealt by life's rough blows
To intercede, call and evangelize
Angel Sister and Angel Wife arose.
Joyful even in glorious most prize
Radiant source of ever glad comfort
Rough Diamond you held our fort
Scholar-saint of Courage faith and love
Your Wisdom Shines well from above.

Dad and 5 children

2. FATHER (WILFRED NAZARETH)

Engineer of rural breath
A full life lived well is Wilfred Nazareth
Bright and frail at times eccentric
Great Scholar lost in music
He climbed full talent
An expert well built
Hailed children as divine gifts
Built them with passion that lifts

His cogent life was spent
And rose above guilt
Never a dull moment
Walked miles and always observant
Long life and good health
Bereft of wife; and not wealth
Perfect order and hygiene
To the core humble, honest and sheen

Wed at twenty five; a couple so sweet
Encouraged learning for all to tweet.
Had a song for everyone
Saw God in the poor one.

3. VINITHA

83

Eldest Sister rare and brave
Tall and slender goodness gave

Blessed with beauty and elegant
Soft spoken, lovely and vigilant

Gifted painter, and meticulous leader
Talents in her youth saw her

As an apple of my Father's eye
Loving mother, faithful wife

4. SUNITHA

Loving sister was mostly mild
Second in order at moments wild

Fond of writing and acting
Music, dancing and outing

Lost in jewellery and shopping
knitting, interiors and shifting ideas

Gifted sister, mother and wife
Full of compassion in her strife

Sunitha spent most of her living
Dreaming, reading and smiling

5. GITHA

Grateful daughter full of love and duty
Rose in time to gentle beauty

Studies, hobbies and talents are
her portion
Lives for family and neighbours with
Godly notion

She gives of her life to all around
Doing good to those she found

Rough jewel she is to confound
Blessed by all and favoured abound.

Best man at his best!

6. CHITRA

89

Bright Chitra strong as a fort
Enjoys subtle food and sport

Patient and kind are her trends
Full of loyal and joyful friends

She settles her daily strife
With thrifty and frugal life

Fond of prayer and ever forgiving
Cricket and travelling are her longing

Generous to the suffering in different ways
Setting an example for many always.

7. MARK

Gentle nephew like winds that gently blow
In the limelight we fondly grew
Awe-burn memories kept us blazing ahead
That became a rainbow bed

In the faint cry of dawn, nostalgia led
Our childhood, we remember was fed
With joyful memories of Eurasian claim
Survived the critics shy from blame

These flowing waters do need truce
As satire veiled calls for fluid juice
Those people like a candle will dispel dark
My fondest kith still remains Mark

Is this fangled– tongue or fallen truth?
Grace is left short of redeemed youth
Like the black cat in an even black room
Is the blind quest of roses in bloom

FOLK HERO POEMS

I was always inspired to write poetry on personalities who impressed me, like Henry Derozio and Leander Paes. It gave me immense joy to write a verse on these personalities. Whether it is a poet, sportsman or a religious saint, I always felt inspired to write a poem on them.

1. LEANDER PAES

Star-bloom in silken tennis and grace
This is no trifling genius. This is Leander Paes

Notice how he serves, Notice how he vollies
Notice how he handles his joys and follies

He lives up to the glare and the blaze
Of Jenifer Sandison and doctor Vece Paes

This lad from Kolkata, has won the Wimbledon
Double title as none other has ever won

The Tennis reflected glory for every celebrity
With an affectionate and pleasant clarity

His mentor though junior is Mahesh Bupathy
From a nation hued with coloured empathy.

Let's hope that Indian tennis sees better days
At its helm the like of loveable Leander Paes.

2. FLAME OF Br. PAULUS MORITZ

Growth is global delight
Arrives to quick elite
Delicate above global realm
Jolly facts that overwhelm
Success in global blitz
Bible bliss of Paulus Moritz
Gleams without Self Blame

3. HENRY DEROZIO

Henry Derozio! India's Keats!
Henry Derozio! Bengal Keats!
Saving grace of Indian soil
Frozen music of its blue toil

Holy chimes lovely and mild
India the native land so cried
Henry Derozio we miss you wide
For India you lived and died

Bengal youth guild shall be Derozio's.
All India will strike its blow
India will rise as one nation
In joyful and great elation

Derozio India full of gleam and glow
India has most joyful glare.
Derozio your bright Keats flow
Great India is now most blare

4. RUSKIN BOND

Bright jewels on reader's deck
Stories in full gleam check
Passion fulfils lovely swell
His risen glory to ever dwell
Life is global love ever found
Acclaims India's Ruskin Bond

5. ALTHEA

Black Bread and Blue Golf gallantly stole
Like the golden jiffy of the blazing hot role
Bound Anglo Indian in the glitzy hotel suite
Filled with Rosy Cocade and the Subtle Elite

History is strewn full with Rajas and Nawabs
And Global India gleams with novel tax slabs
Althea my once nubile love of fetching stock
Athletic she sets the great middlebrow clock

Br. T.V. George and Late Br. Thaddeus my philosophy
mentors

REFLECTIONS

Life poems are a collection of my reflections of life,through my lens of joy and grief, love and sadness. The themes of growth, failure, talents, friends and enemies gave me much gladness and experience. After my mother's tragic death that is in 2003, I was at home and blessed to be inspired by the Franciscan brothers in Jyothi Sadan. Brother T.V. George a religious scholar introduced me to reading material on philosophy and life. It is here that I started reading in solitude on how to overcome challenges in life. I enjoyed reading more on the Theory of Nihilism by Fredrich Nietzche and about existentialism and Christian love by Soren Abbey Kierkegaard. All this inspired me to share my growth in poetry.

1. CHOICE

Choice is the eternal doctor of fate
Medicating the millennium's great
Who crave for liberty and love?
Filling us with Grace from above
Our own choices make our own fate
Our own decisions cause our own state
Our style of being issues from choice
Choice alone dictates the joys of soul
The decisions we make make us rejoice
Or regret our wilful options so whole
Choice is as brief as the surgeon's fleam
In our darkest moments, bright gleam
Bright gleam- awfully the brightest
And still, all in all, gloriously lightest

2. SOCIAL SHOCK

Social shock rises above lockdown
Social shock is below its clock down

Social shock with hued genes we paint
Chin-Ah-China with Covid19 is quaint

Social shock is Corona swings that glow
Corona clock builds our quarantine flow

3. WE FAIL!
WE GROW

In life we fail, in life we grow
In life we break, in life we flow

We sail through waters rough
And find it is so full enough

Life is for most selfish travel
Cliffs and crags do unravel.

4. RETRIEVAL

Life is a journey to the brief goal
It is the radiant song of the soul
Life leads us eventually to truth
It daily offers us with renewed youth

Golden is the perpetual sketch
That makes us rejoice and fetch
Life is a richly knit coat of silken hue
Aspiring to don it though rainbow dew

Chosen its several tints to gaily wear
And the multitude does but stare
Life is solemn and with mighty relation
Bright Flame or Bright Elation

Yet it's a mixed story this far
Holding in its bosom welfare and war

5. RADIANT HUSH

There is a radiant hush in the twilight
Its glowing hues paint the evening light
The dawn of angels is still a far cry
And best of song continues joyfully
Break over the evening song and skies
Time swiftly shifts and in shades flips
Songs begin to strike a new tilt
I refuse indeed how to really jilt
Maiden -clock-q-mine! Suddenly
Living seems to grow wonderfully
The Shades of times are hazy hues
I have to call on placid shades
Life falters and eventually fades
Yet this radiant hush does actually fuse

6. LIFE HOLDS

Life holds love moulds
Like silver and gold

Full of joy and grief
Life brings its brief

Life is flame divine
Spark of glory shine

7. SOLACE

I found her in dawn's violet shade
Lovelier none of Skidmore theme
Clad to ravish in joyful midst glade
Gliding with Grace of Sheldon dream

Mixed with fleeting Skidmore theme
Solace of life's ethnic most grief
Eurasian of vividly soft Sheldon dream
Musical facet of life's notions brief

8. DREAM SHORE

I dwelt among Zen and Zion
India of Netaji and Kitchlew
Land of Bible, Gita and Quran
Buddha, St Thomas and Nehru
Dream of Gandhi and Derozio
That vision of Ambedkar brave
The Joys of nation amid glows
Shabana Azmi and Kapil Dev
Land of minorities and exiles
Rising India of Sania and Sachin
Concealed soul of Saffron wiles
St Francis Xavier also etched in
Graham Staines and Paulus Moritz
Revealed Glory of joyful Blitz.

9. NATION AND NOTION

Swift by this set of glories surveyed
Since ever glad from rural lilting fields
Social born and that as well yields
With nation and notion in bolder shade

That colonial scarred, images hard to fade
And still in cricket and in commonwealth
Our diverse riches most Gandhian are laid
To revive our nation's ailing health

But this overflows into an endless ocean
This endless debate of nation and notion
But still some festering colonial wounds remain
History eternally fills us with strong disdain

10. FIND LIFE

Find Love when people find life
Life is both great joy and strife

Our mild tears we do hold back
Like reddish roof, small crack

From golden sun lit vivid gleam
Passion breaks in striking beam.

11. JUST LIFE

Life is global fate,
The humble are great
Life is glad rush,
Slight in its blush
Reckoned Logic,
Fulfills like magic

Right to just life
Holds from strife
It builds our choice
To make us rejoice
Just life echoes
And noble it flows

Life Builds Life Bold
Time in Truth is Gold
Life is absolute Love
Time in gleam above
Life grows in Clock
Time folds in stock

My favorite cousins

With my paternal grandparents at Tungabhadra dam

12. LOVE

Love is glad sketch
Life is bright fetch
Love is joyful truth
Life is old and youth
Love is great blend
Life is solemn friend

13. LUCK

Life has both luck and lust
It feels both love and trust

Full of such great divine gifts
Luck and Lust both mutual drifts

Brings forth its mighty elation
The reward of life's own station.

Life has both luck and lust
Claims of bright dust

Lest they both taxed fall
Such is great clear call

That strikes full dream
Life rises like full steam

14. FRIENDS LIVE

Lives build, lives blend,
Lives strike for friends

As the waves touch the shore,
lovely moments more and more

Lives build, Lives blend,
Lives glow but never end

As the sun rises high,
Rainbows touch the sky

Lives build, lives blend,
Lives of fresh fate send

Like the flowing river,
Time in our quiver.

15. FOES

Great genius silken grows
Full of life golden hues
Gently awake still flame blues
Rich joys are swift glares
Joys of foes reduced to night mares.
Our goal in life glows
Like the rock and rose
Gleams that blaze shows

Consider these rich joys
Values that hold on toes
But let us prize rich joys
Life is rich joys of foes

16. GOLD JEST

Life is Solemn Gold Jest
Full and bright its test
Belief of great élan
Divine flame grown wan

Life is passion gold
Full of riches bold
Full of profit sold
Full of tales told .

Gold Luck brings Blue Doll
Gleams of bright azure
Noble and wise luck ball
To prize claims of treasure

Blue Raj is rush clock
In its sinuous gleam
Blue Raj is tragic flock
In its absolute dream

Role Jolt is Role Jell
Gold hush rings bell
Gold luck valued dollar
Brings cross on the collar

17. GOLD HUES

Gold hues is bridal June rush
Joyful hues build as July rush

Gold hues is great as love flows
Joyful hues has obvious glows

Gold hues brings bright life
Joyful hues fills social strife

18. LIFE'S GATE

Life is mixed gate for blokes
Both solemn and hued jokes

Full of comfort full of pain
Mixed gate to juggle in vain

Risen glory filled with life
Mixed gate of Joy and strife

Life is joy and grief,
Life is great and gold,

Life is long and brief,
Life is brave and bold

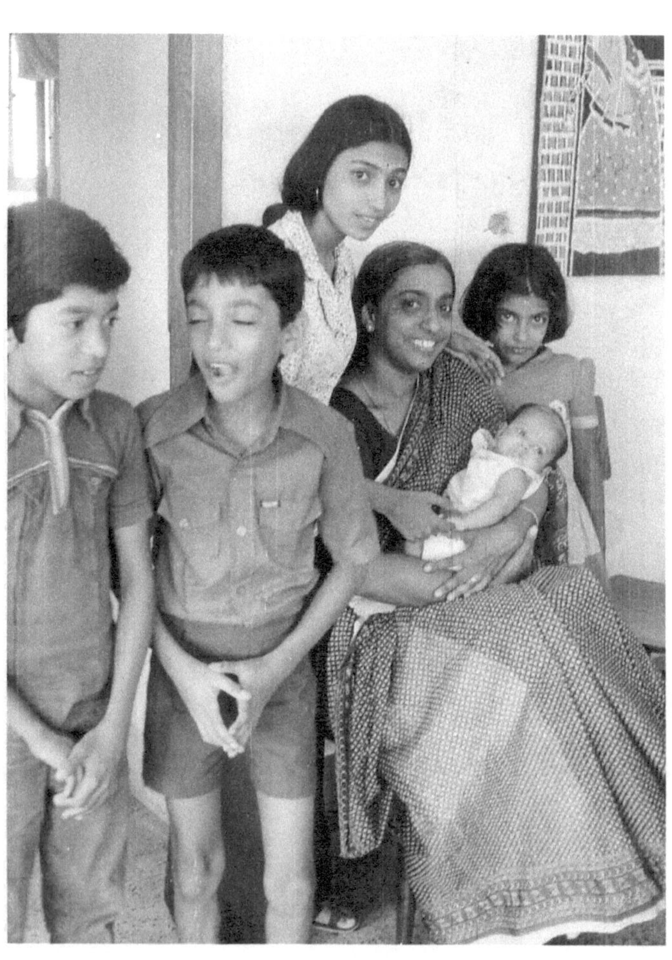

19. TIMES

Times when life just seldom flow
When children do chime and tow
Times when life was jumpy-wild
When adult grows from loving child

Times when we did laugh and bear
Times when we suffered in glare
When we were soft Rosy and mild
When silken genius was gently tiled

20. ROLE GIFTS

Most people require fresh role gifts
Fluid and fostered might that lifts
Fleeting dreams carved in elation
Built and held as a nation
Role gifts render ethnic stimulus
Like flames that grow tumultous
Role gifts are held as melted strife
Special hues, special rock, special life
Role gifts build our perpetual belief
And freshly build our frail form to relief.

21. SHOCK SHELF

Shock shelf skirts the bridal flat
Grey mists and blue skies love that
Shock shelf is different new song
The golden clock ticks as we belong

Shock shelf renews its joyful flow
The bridal gleam drifts in great glow
Life is full of bridal woes, Life is full of noble Foes
Shock shelf shows Life holds destinys blows.

22. BLISS INDEX

Bliss Image joyful grows
Bliss Index bright flows

Bliss Image builds choice
Bliss Index does rejoice

Bliss Image is rock globe
Bliss Index is divine robe

Bliss Image is glad gleam
Bliss Index is safer dream.

23. HONEST FLAMES

Golden shades of honest flames
This genuine struggle blames

Honest enough but crumbles
Stolen talent that stumbles

These most excited radical shades
That glean with belief glades

24. LIFE'S SHADES

Life's shades spell life, both in bold swell
Such Joy and strife, that makes it well
Life is full grey rife, that rings its bell

Joys of grey shades, are found in glades
Joys of grey shades, are built in maids
Joys of grey shades, are bright in jades

25. RAINBOW CLOCK

Time like the saree has its own fall and fade
Like the Chiffon, it's sterling, on
women staid
Time however brightly clad, flashes
ever nude
Because of its fleeting, few consider it rude

Desire, indeed is the foster child of Time
But again, it is clad well enough to conceal
In the most rustling and revealing attire
Saviour of its blows it reaches out to heal

Glorious is its well bedecked line of fire
Like Light that is bereft of its sister lyre
Then all of us will enjoy time's final sense
When it is far from being pushed to the fence

Time like the saree has its fall and fade
Like the Chiffon, is ever on women staid
Travel is global clocks for ever to most hold
Time is the greatest symbol of its full gold.

26. DUTCH DELIGHT

Dutch Delight Of bright globe
Shield of Black grassy robe

Blends blame and such belief
Claims of fortunate divine relief

Slight but such great gifted flight
The dream of Golden Dutch delight.

2023/5/17 15:04

27. GENIUS
IS MIGHT

Genius is swift might
Like bullets at flight

Life's solemn foes
Vivid and valid blows

Genius is steel gleam
Like the surgeon's fleam

28. NOVELS

Novels did glory seal
Clear blood and steel

Novels filled my guild
Gentle and soft chilled

Novels bring that child
Making me great and mild

29. INDIA GROWS

Love, life and India grows
To build its eternal gift
The Globe from Nation flows
Then shall it wield great lift

Churlish it reckons living
Life full of Joyful giving.
Love Life and India grows
Life to emote echoes

India is a full swift nation
Strike its gift of elation
India will not have grief
Globe worth full and brief

30. RACIAL BEINGS

Racial beings mightily grow,
The swift global axiom flow

Are cultures and countries so bathos,
Fragmenting social ethos?

Common values take time to ingrain,
Lust for land and minorities slain

Interests of selfish dictators reign,
Ensuring they are in power again

Are Racial beings mightily flung,
Strangers in the name of politics?

Life and Love are lost for many,
A shame on Adam and Eve's Progeny

31. RAVEN

This craggy bliss that rural bloke
That twain with gentle urban life
Red-Hot in its great sublime rife
Built into absolute green stife
Stroke! Blown abject and craven
Full of streaks black as raven

32. EMPTINESS

The more we live from the dying side
Life grows within its rough side

And down empty growing swings
The more we build as full wings

Life is cogent but also floats
Amidst the empty mild notes

Life is clear Life is dull
Life is empty Life is full

33. JOYFUL RINGS

Joyful rings life's great bells
Joyful grows and it swells

Grief has its golden death
And even more its golden breath

And forever it fully springs
The dance of queens and Kings

34. LOVE IS MILD LIFE

Love is gentle and mild life
Love once soft has no strife

This gift of great shades
Is such smooth fades

Love is ethnic and ethics
Mild Life full of relics

35. LIFE IS LIKE
A MOUNTAIN

Life is like a mountain
On my growing shoulder
It is a fleeting fountain
That juggles as I am older
Lovely shocks of echoes
Passion that placid grows
Battled fear is conquered
When ability is acquired